How Is Jesus Different
from Other
Religious Leaders?

Ralph O. Muncaster

HARVEST HOUSE PUBLISHERS
Eugene, Oregon 97402

Cover by Terry Dugan Design, Minneapolis, Minnesota

A Special Thanks to Karen Bell-Wilcox for her endless hours spent contributing to the perspectives in this book and for her ministry contribution. Karen is a major leader in Strong Basis to Believe Ministries and has been involved in the research of several ministry topics. Karen is a CPA with a master's degree in business administration and has also pursued advanced studies in such diverse sciences as chemistry, biology, and physics.

By Ralph O. Muncaster

Are There Hidden Codes in the Bible?
Can Archaeology Prove the New Testament?
Can Archaeology Prove the Old Testament?
Can We Know for Certain We Are Going to Heaven?
Can You Trust the Bible?
Creation vs. Evolution
Creation vs. Evolution Video
Does Prayer Really Work?
Does the Bible Predict the Future?
How to Talk About Jesus with the Skeptics in Your Life
How Do We Know Jesus is God?
Is the Bible Really a Message from God?
Science—Was the Bible Ahead of Its Time?
What Is the Proof for the Resurrection?
What is the Trinity?
How Is Jesus Different from Other Religious Leaders?
What Really Happened Christmas Morning?
What Really Happens When You Die?
Why Does God Allow Suffering?

HOW IS JESUS DIFFERENT FROM OTHER RELIGIOUS LEADERS?
Examine the Evidence Series

Copyright © 2001 by Ralph O. Muncaster
Published by Harvest House Publishers
Eugene, Oregon 97402

Library of Congress Cataloging-in-Publication Data

Muncaster, Ralph O.
  How is Jesus different from other religious leaders? / Ralph O. Muncaster.
     p. cm. — (Examine the evidence series)
  Includes bibliographical references.
  ISBN 0-7369-0612-6
     1. Jesus Christ—Person and offices. 2. Christianity and other religions. 3. Apologetics.
  I. Title

BT203 .M86 2001
232—dc21   00-053956

Printed in the United States of America.

01 02 03 04 05 06 07 08 09 10 / BP / 10 9 8 7 6 5 4 3 2 1

Contents

What's So Important About a Religious Leader?

Religion is, by one of its basic definitions, "belief in and reverence for a supernatural power accepted as the creator and governor of the universe."[1]

If we accept that such a "supernatural power" exists, and if we assume that we might need to show "reverence" for him, her, or it, then it makes sense to take our relationship to such a god seriously. After all, if this god had the power to create us, then he, she, or it must very likely also have the power to destroy us or otherwise determine our destiny.

Since various religions often present opposing views about the "supernatural power" and other issues, *they cannot all be true.* Selecting the religious worldview that conforms to the way things actually are is of the ultimate importance. It could literally mean the difference between eternal paradise or eternal torment—let alone its effect on our quality of life while we are on earth. So it's vitally important to investigate religions *before* we select a path.*

One major part of the investigation of religions must be the examination of religious leaders, who define and interpret doctrine—beliefs— for their followers. These leaders include such infamous figures as Jim Jones, who ordered the Jonestown mass suicide; David Koresh, leader of the militaristic Branch Davidians in Waco, Texas; and Marshall Applewhite, who inspired the mass suicide of the Heaven's Gate group. Obviously, religious leaders can be very dangerous right here on earth!

Those leaders who are potentially even more dangerous are those who have founded the world's largest religions. If some of them are wrong, and only one is right, then the *eternal destinies* of billions of their followers lie in the balance.

Careful, thorough analysis will reveal, beyond a shadow of a doubt, that Jesus is the only religious leader who has provided ample evidence and reason to trust all of His words. Examining the evidence for choosing Him is by far the most important act of your life—worth taking time away from TV, vacations, the Internet, and other activities. This book will help guide your analysis of key religious leaders and will help define what sets Jesus and biblical Christianity apart from all other religions and religious leaders.

* The objective of the entire *Examine the Evidence* series is to give help in judging the evidence for faith.

The Key Issues

1.
What Is the Role of the Leader?

Since the leader, and especially the founder, of a religion defines doctrine or beliefs, it is critical to understand the role he or she assumes in that religion. (See pages 6–13.)

2.
What Are the Claims of the Leader?

The claims of a leader (or a religion) provide an obvious starting point for analysis. It will be by these claims that the validity of the leader will ultimately be tested. (See pages 8, 9, 14–43.)

3.
Can We Confirm the Claims?

It is vital that a leader's key claims be subject to confirmation. Is there adequate support for the claims, or are they just rhetorical statements—or even deliberate falsehoods? (See pages 8–11, 14–43.)

4.
Do Actions Support the Claims?

If a leader's claims are legitimate and sincere, we should expect to see actions that support and are consistent with the doctrine or beliefs. (See pages 14–43.)

5.
Is There Divine Confirmation?

Assuming that a religious leader is selected or appointed by God, there should be supernatural evidence that confirms God's involvement. (See pages 14–43.)

Analyzing Religious Leaders' Roles

Religious leaders assume many roles. It's important to understand the role that a leader plays within a religion so that we can evaluate him or her from the right perspective. Does a leader maintain that he possesses unique insight into ancient holy books? Does he say that he is a prophet? Does he say that he is a god? These three roles are very different.

Leaders should be evaluated by their claims. Assuming that the leaders we are considering are human, we can evaluate their roles within a religion by using the following criteria:

1. Do they claim to authoritatively interpret something old?

2. Do they proclaim something new?

3. Do they claim divine insight?

4. Do they claim to be God (or a god)?

It's important to consider the priority of these roles. For instance, merely *interpreting* something is obviously less important than actually *being* God. However, even more important is the central issue—*can the person prove his or her claims?* Hence, in our analysis of roles and claims, it will be important to look both at what is claimed and at the strength of the evidence that supports those claims. Someone who maintains that he is God *and can prove it* should carry far more weight with us—and is far more worthy of our attention—than someone who simply claims to interpret ancient holy writings.

> We are entitled to evaluate our religious leaders.
> In fact, we *must* evaluate them—
> our eternity may be at stake.

Priority of Leaders' Roles
(Lowest to Highest)

1. Do they interpret something old?

2. Do they proclaim something new?

3. Do they claim divine insight?

4. Do they claim to be God?

Many religious leaders claim several of the above roles. But how far is a leader willing to go in *committing* to his or her claim? Is he only a gifted interpreter, or is he a god? Once we determine the extent of the leader's claim, we can proceed to analyze whether or not there is *adequate evidence to satisfy the claim.*

We can give priority only to those claims that have adequate evidence to support them.

In the end, we will discover this:

Jesus is unique, in that He claimed to be God—and proved it.
No one else made such an extreme claim.
No one else has such a weight of evidence in support of his claim—
even though that claim might be a far lesser one.

Claims—and Their Confirmation

The claims of any religious leader are of paramount importance to his or her authority. For instance, a person may profess to be "enlightened" and propose speculative ideas that can never be tested; all of it may amount to a pleasing philosophy, but it's a weak claim—nearly anyone can do it.

On the other hand, if a person proclaims that he is God and can prove it by performing miracles unequaled by anyone else— ever—then that person has a very strong claim.

So when we analyze the claims of religious leaders, we need to ask:

1. Is the claim special or remarkable?

A claim to be God in human flesh is *very* special. A claim to be a great interpreter of some holy writing is an assertion that anyone can make. (See "Priority of Leaders' Roles" on page 7.)

2. Is the claim verifiable?

Some people profess to be prophets—but many of them speak only of the distant future or the end of the world. Thus their predictions can never be tested. They are not verifiable. On the other hand, prophets who display accuracy in their prediction of *events that later occur and can be witnessed* are making claims that can be confirmed. Any end-time prophecies spoken by such people are much more likely to be reliable.

3. Is there evidence of divine confirmation?

Many people purport to be divinely appointed and approved. But is their divine appointment verifiable? Is there substantive evidence that a leader is truly endorsed by God? Are there just empty words, or is there an indication that those words have a supernatural being's stamp of approval?

4. Do the actions and the ultimate fate of the leader support his or her claims?

We often say, "Talk is cheap." People who espouse a philosophy but then go against it themselves are hypocrites. Those who imply they have one of the roles of a religious leader but do not fulfill that role are fakes. And people who predict something that does not come to pass are false prophets.

Confirming Religious Leaders and Their Doctrine

We must ask the questions above before we can endorse any religious leader. Otherwise we face the possibility of being misled in a decision that will affect us for eternity. Some further, practical questions to ask might be:

1. Is the religion based on *untestable philosophy* or on *historical events*?

2. Is there some undeniable fact about the religion that reveals *divine confirmation,* such as perfect prediction of the future?

3. Are the daily words and actions of a religious leader *consistent* with the proclamations he or she makes and the beliefs he or she espouses?

Analyzing the Actions of Leaders

The following pages give a brief look at the history, doctrine, and confirmation (or lack of it) of some of the most prominent religious leaders and founders of religions. The list is far from all-inclusive, but it provides a basic model for the evaluation of religious leaders.

Sometimes we forget how profoundly leaders influence people. Apart from the leaders mentioned earlier, whose excesses brought disaster to their followers, consider the Pope, Billy Graham, or Muhammad. And if we trace our way forward from the time of some of the founders of the world's most prominent religions, we find that these leaders have shaped the belief systems of hundreds of millions of people—over thousands of years.

Here is a graphic model of the basic interaction between a religious leader and his followers.

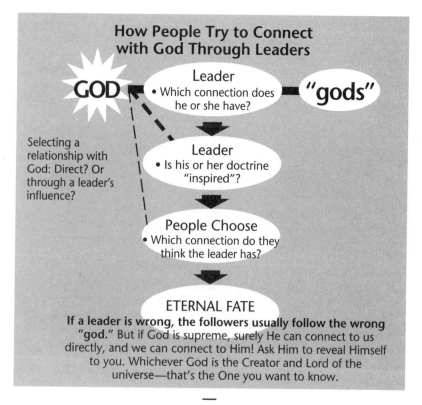

How People Try to Connect with God Through Leaders

GOD

Leader
• Which connection does he or she have?

"gods"

Selecting a relationship with God: Direct? Or through a leader's influence?

Leader
• Is his or her doctrine "inspired"?

People Choose
• Which connection do they think the leader has?

ETERNAL FATE

If a leader is wrong, the followers usually follow the wrong "god." But if God is supreme, surely He can connect to us directly, and we can connect to Him! Ask Him to reveal Himself to you. Whichever God is the Creator and Lord of the universe—that's the One you want to know.

Religious leaders always imply that they have a spiritual connection with the real "God," whether this is true or not. And they always imply that their doctrine or philosophy is inspired by "God," whether true or not. People are then "inspired" by these religious leaders, who often lead them on a path to a false god.

But anyone can talk to God directly and ask for the truth; God will lead anyone to the true path. Anyone can ask:

1. "Direct me to the truth, no matter what it is."

2. "Reveal to me the way You communicate to me and what Your message is."

3. "Let me know the real 'God,' not some human idea of who 'God' is."

Leaders of World Religions in History

The chart on the next page shows some of the world religious leaders who have had the greatest impact in history. All of them have led millions of people to a belief in a "god" (or "gods")—whether right or wrong. For each of them, we must assess:

1. Whether the "god" (or "gods") each leader promotes is real and true.

2. Whether the leader is a legitimate spokesman for God.

3. What the one true God actually wants us to do.

The Heritage of Major Leaders of World Religions

Judaism—Judaism is too small to be called a "world religion." Its adherents make up less than one percent of the world's population (fewer than some religions that are not listed here). However, the impact of Judaism has been enormous because it is the foundation of the Christian religion (Jesus was Jewish) and is largely the basis for Islam.

Christianity—The largest world religion, with about a third of the world's population, it quickly spread within the eastern hemisphere during the time after the resurrection of Jesus Christ. It is history-based (based on historical facts and events).

Islam—Founded by Muhammad, Islam combines much of Judaism (several of the books of the Hebrew Scriptures—the "Old Testament"), Christianity (a version of the gospel), and adds the writings based on Muhammad's teaching (the Qur'an). About 20 percent of the world's population adheres to Islam.

Hinduism—The other foundational world religion, Hinduism, has adherents that number about 13 percent of the world's population. It is philosophy-based (that is, it is based on ideas, not on historical facts and events) and has no known single founder.

Buddhism—Founded by Buddha after a period of "enlightenment," it is a reconstruction of the fundamentals of the Hindu religion and is likewise philosophy-based. About six percent of the world's population follows Buddhism.

Confucianism—Confucius was the originator of the philosophies that were formed into the Confucian religion. Three to four percent of the world's population follows Confucianism. It also is a philosophy-based religion.

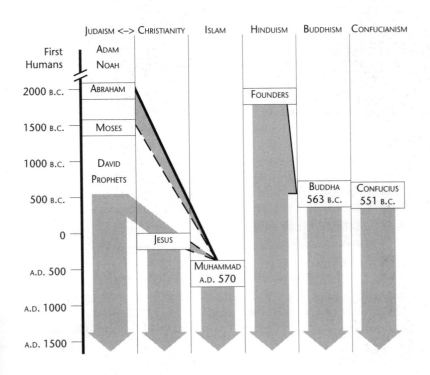

The Founders and Leaders of Judaism

Judaism is the foundation of the history-based religions of Christianity and Islam, which together claim more than 50 percent of the world's population. Hence, even though the followers of Judaism are relatively few (less than one percent of the world's population), it is an extremely important religion, as are its founders and leaders who are described in the Bible.

Abraham

Abraham was unique because he was called by the God of the universe to go to the land of Canaan (Palestine—now mostly modern Israel) to be the "father" of a nation. The people of this nation would become God's messengers to carry His Word to all mankind. God promised a child to Abraham and his wife, Sarah, despite their age (each of them was about 100 years old—beyond childbearing age). After a number of years passed without fulfillment of this promise, the couple decided to fulfill it themselves without God's involvement. Sarah gave her servant, Hagar, to Abraham as a "concubine" (a wife of secondary status). This union produced the child Ishmael, whom the Arab nations claim as their father. And it is among the Arabs that Islam was founded and has its greatest strength.

Later Abraham and Sarah were blessed with the miracle child God had promised—Isaac—who became the father of the nation of Israel. The line of Isaac's descendants led to Jesus, who claimed to be the long-promised Messiah whose coming was predicted by the prophets of Israel. (These prophecies are recorded in the Books of the Prophets in the Hebrew Scriptures—the "Old Testament.")

Jesus is the foundation of Christianity. He is also claimed by Islam—as one of their greatest prophets. Thus the two major history-based religions of the world, Christianity and Islam—whose adherents together represent more than 50 percent of the world's population—rest upon this single historical person.

Moses

Moses is considered by some people to be the founder of Judaism. Under the inspiration of God, he wrote the *Torah*—the first five books of the Hebrew Scriptures—which is the foundation for Judaism.

Moses did *not* claim to be a god, but merely a messenger who transmitted words from God. The key evidence in support of his claim to divine appointment is his prophecy—perfectly fulfilled in history, no prophecies ever wrong, even though some of his predictions were made hundreds of years in advance of the actual events.

The Basic Doctrine of Judaism*

God: There is one God, who created the universe and everything in it.

Mankind: People are separated from God by sin.

Sin: People are sinful, but can be reconciled to God by making sacrifices for their sin.

Eternity: People can gain an eternal dwelling with God by following the laws of Moses.

Key Leaders:	Abraham Moses David The prophets
Period:	2000 B.C. to 400 B.C.
Holy Writings:	The Hebrew Scriptures (The "Old Testament" of the Bible)
Key Claims*:	One God Mankind is sinful Jews selected by God Salvation by works
Key Evidence:	Archaeology and history
Divine Evidence:	Fulfilled prophecy in the "Books of the Prophets" and the "Books of Moses"

*The three major branches of Judaism differ on specific doctrines.

Jesus (Christianity)

Jesus is the foundation of the Christian faith. Apart from His teaching, He made a claim that was far more special—something that no other major religious leader asserted:

He claimed to be God in human form.

Jesus fits precisely with the Jewish beliefs about a coming *Messiah** (literally, the "anointed one [anointed by God]"). These beliefs are not new—they are built firmly upon the words of the Old Testament of the Bible. In turn, Jesus' teaching supports Abraham, Moses, and the entire Hebrew Scriptures. He personally fulfills the prophecies given in these Scriptures. And Christianity is founded upon his life, death, and resurrection, all of which are historically documented events.

Jesus' life and words often gave clues that would help people recognize that He was God in human form. For instance, the manner, circumstances, and location of His birth all fulfilled ancient prophecies—and they were just the beginning of the record of divine evidence in support of His claims. Jesus' earthly father, Joseph, had been given a dream to confirm that Jesus would be called "Immanuel" (Matthew 1:23), which means "God with us"—just as had been predicted by the prophet Isaiah (Isaiah 7:14). Furthermore, throughout His public life, Jesus Himself showed that His claim to be God was true by 1) performing miracles that "only God could perform" and 2) perfectly fulfilling His own prophecy of His death and resurrection (see pages 40, 41).

These miracles, these prophecies, and their fulfillment are recorded in thousands of surviving copies of documents that were written by eyewitnesses to the events surrounding Jesus' life: the Gospels of the New Testament. The Gospels are written accounts of the same evidence that Jesus presented personally to the people of His time. All of these documents withstood the test of scrutiny by eyewitnesses of Jesus' life.

The Basic Doctrine of Jesus (Christianity)

God: There is one God. Jesus is the Son—one of the three "Persons" of the three-in-one Godhead (Father, Son, and Holy Spirit).

Mankind: People are

---

*The word "Christ" comes from the Greek word that means the same thing as the Hebrew word *messiah*.

sinful by nature.

Sin: People are separated from God by sin, and must accept God's gift of Jesus' sacrifice on their behalf in order to be reconciled with God.

Eternity: Eternity is a gift from God, given freely to people as a result of their committing themselves to Jesus.

Leader:	Jesus
Active Period:	A.D. 30 to A.D. 33
Holy Writings:	The Bible—the Old Testament
	The Bible—the New Testament
Key Claims:	Jesus claimed to be God
	Everyone is sinful and needs redemption
	Jesus is the Redeemer
	Salvation is by grace —God's gift
Key Evidence:	Prophecy, history, archaeology
Divine Evidence:	Extraordinary prophecy
	Resurrection from death

Jesus' Teaching

The Greatest Commandment—"Love the Lord your God with all your heart and with all your soul and with all your mind and all your strength" (Mark 12:30).

The Second Greatest Commandment—"Love your neighbor as [in the same way you love] yourself" (Mark 12:31).

The New Commandment—"Love one another. *As I have loved you,* so you must love one another. By this all men will know that you are my disciples, if you love one another" (John 13:34, emphasis added).

Jesus' Great Commission—"Make disciples of all men, baptizing them in the name of the Father, the Son, and the Holy Spirit [the triune God]; and teaching them to obey everything I have commanded you. And surely I am with you always, to the very end of the age" (Matthew 28:19,20).

The Fate of Jesus:
Jesus was crucified in A.D. 32 or 33. He *rose from the dead,* an event attested to by hundreds of people. He Himself now lives *in the hearts of people* who have committed themselves to Him.

Muhammad (Islam)

Muhammad is the founder of Islam, whose followers (called Muslims) make up about 20 percent of the world's population.[2,3] (The Arabic word *islam* means "submission [to the will of God].") Some Islamic beliefs were influenced by the Jewish Scriptures (the Old Testament of the Bible) or the Christian New Testament—both Judaism and Christianity were highly influential in the region where Muhammad started his work. Muhammad is considered by Muslims to be the ultimate prophet, above Jesus, Moses, and others.

History[3,4,5]

Islam is the third of the major history-based religions, after Judaism and Christianity. None of these three religions denies the historical existence of Abraham, Moses, David, Jesus, or Muhammad. Only the teachings and actions of each person are in dispute.

Muhammad was born in A.D. 570, into an Arabian tribe that controlled the important trade city of Mecca. Local custom called for every spiritual person to go to a "place of solitude" once a year to pay homage to various gods. Muhammad alleged that, in one such experience that he had at age 40, the angel Gabriel had given him his first revelation about the one single God—Allah. This revelation gave him insights that later became the basis of the writings of the Qur'an.

Muhammad doubted this first revelation because monotheism (belief in one single God) was not common or popular in the region. As time went on, other people convinced him to become bolder; and his preaching about monotheism eventually resulted in his expulsion from Mecca. He embraced both Christianity and Judaism to a degree, and though he was later rejected, the Qur'an actually contains much material from extrabiblical Jewish sources and from heretical "Christian" writings such as the *Gospel of Thomas*.[17] In the year 630 he returned triumphantly to Mecca, taking control without a struggle, and began to institute his new religion of Islam.

The Teaching of Islam[3,4,5]

Major Groups: Sunni Muslims (about 80 percent of Muslims) recognize only written traditions as authoritative. Shi'ite Muslims also recognize the authority of certain living people. The groups disagree over who the rightful successors to Muhammad were.

God: God is a single unit. Considering Jesus and the Holy Spirit to be God is blasphemous.

Mankind: People are by nature good.

Sin: People can be forgiven of sin through repentance. Jesus' involvement is not necessary.

Jesus: Jesus is a great prophet, but to identify Him as God is blasphemous.

Leader:	Muhammad
Dates:	A.D. 570 to 632
Holy Writings:	The Qur'an
	The Bible—the Torah and Psalms (revised)
	The Bible—the Gospels (revised)
Key Claims:	One God—Allah
	The prophets of God include: Adam, Noah, Abraham, Moses, David, Solomon, Jonah, John the Baptist, Jesus, Muhammad
Key Prophet:	Muhammad
Key Evidence:	History
Divine Evidence:	The "beauty" of the Qur'an

Salvation: People are saved by virtue of their deeds. Their good deeds must outweigh their bad deeds at the day of judgment.

Leadership Issues

Muhammad seemed to be receptive to Christians and Jews until they rejected him. Among other things, this caused him to turn from Jerusalem to Mecca as the most holy city. This raises the question as to how much of Muhammad's theology was a reaction to Judaism and Christianity, as opposed to revelation from God.

The Fate of Muhammad:
Muhammad died on June 8, 632 and remained dead.

Confucius (Confucianism)

China, with its large population, is the home of several of the largest Eastern world religions: Confucianism, Taoism, and their variations, all of which are philosophy-based. Confucianism remains strong today, but Taoism has greatly waned during the Communist era in China. Of the philosophy-based religions in the Far East, Confucianism claims the most followers.

History[3,4,5]

Confucius* lived during the sixth and fifth centuries B.C., about the time of Buddha. His teachings gained popularity during the decline of Taoism, a ritual-based religion that had previously been widespread in China. Confucius taught moral laws, not just rituals. As Confucianism spread and became dominant, it was often combined with the practice of Buddhism, as it still is today.

The Teaching of Confucius[3,4,5]

Summary: Confucianism is essentially a set of moral-philosophical beliefs. For this reason, many people do not consider it a religion.

God: He (it) is not really personal, but is the ultimate reality. Confucius himself did not profess to be divine, though some sects later deified him.

Mankind: People are good by nature and are potentially perfect.

Sin: Sin only occurs when people are forced to act in evil ways, or when they allow their minds to wander to evil thoughts.

Jesus: Jesus has no bearing on Confucian thought.

Salvation: There is no precise definition. It is sometimes viewed as a creative moral power or an impersonal principle.

* The name "Confucius" is a Latin form of the Chinese name "K'ung-Fu-tzu."

Leadership Issues

Confucius was more of a politician than a religious leader. He held many official positions and was able to convince many of his contemporaries that his moral-political system was the best way to restructure Chinese society. His wisdom was revered and his sayings were well known, but they remained mostly in the philosophical arena (much like the teachings of Socrates and Plato, who were active not long after Confucius' time). After Confucius' death, some of his followers began to venerate him as divine.[4,6]

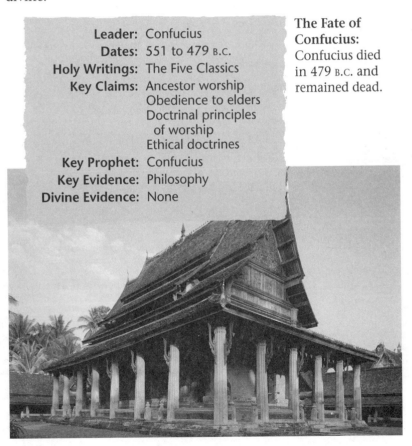

Leader:	Confucius
Dates:	551 to 479 B.C.
Holy Writings:	The Five Classics
Key Claims:	Ancestor worship
	Obedience to elders
	Doctrinal principles
	of worship
	Ethical doctrines
Key Prophet:	Confucius
Key Evidence:	Philosophy
Divine Evidence:	None

The Fate of Confucius: Confucius died in 479 B.C. and remained dead.

Comparison of Some...

Leader (Religion)	Significance of Key Claims	Verifiability of Key Claims
Abraham (Judaism)	**Claim:** God chose him to be the father of a great nation. **Significance:** ●●●	**Evidence:** Jewish writings. Some archaeology. Jesus' references. **Rating:** ●●●●
Moses (Judaism)	**Claim:** God chose him to teach the world about His nature and His law. **Significance:** ●●●●	**Evidence:** Jewish writings. History. Archaeology. Jesus' references. **Rating:** ●●●●●
Jesus (Christianity)	**Claim:** *He is in fact God* in human form. **Significance:** ●●●●●●●	**Evidence:** Eyewitnesses, martyrs, manuscripts, history, archaeology. **Rating:** ●●●●●●●
Muhammad (Islam)	**Claim:** God chose him to be a prophet greater than Moses and Jesus. **Significance:** ●●●●●	**Evidence:** Islamic writings. Some archaeology. History. Disciples. **Rating:** ●●●●●
Confucius (Confucianism)	**Claim:** He had "political insight" and wisdom beyond others. **Significance:** ●	**Evidence:** Totally philosophy—cannot produce evidence. **Rating:** -
Hindu Leaders (Hinduism)	**Claim:** They had philosophical wisdom about the gods and about eternity. **Significance:** ●	**Evidence:** No direct evidence that the philosophies are "correct." **Rating:** ●
Buddha (Buddhism)	**Claim:** He became "enlightened" beyond Hindus in his philosophy. **Significance:** ●●	**Evidence:** Tradition from followers. Nothing supports his claims as "correct." **Rating:** ●
Joseph Smith (Mormonism)	**Claim:** He is a god equal to Jesus, and God gave him a "special" message. **Significance:** ●●●●●●●	**Evidence:** None. **Rating:** -
Charles Russell (Jehovah's Witnesses)	**Claim:** God chose him with "special" prophetic revelation. **Significance:** ●●	**Evidence:** None. Even some followers have rejected his teachings. **Rating:** -
Mary Baker Eddy (Christian Science)	**Claim:** She had philosophical insight into interpreting the Bible. **Significance:** ●	**Evidence:** None. Her doctrine about medicine has led to many deaths. **Rating:** -
L. Ron Hubbard (Scientology)	**Claim:** He had "special insight" into "knowing" the universe and eternity. **Significance:** ●	**Evidence:** This "religion" has caused many kinds of problems. **Rating:** -

SIGNIFICANCE RATINGS
The significance ratings are simply an encouragement to readers to use their own judgment when weighing the claims made by religious leaders or the degree to which they are supported by evidence. Opinions may vary on the judgments that have been made above. But objective analysis indicates that there is a relation between the significance of a leader's claim and the significance of the leader himself. For example, someone who simply contends that he has philosophical insight (such as Confucius) has a less significant claim than someone who professes to have specific guidance from God (such as Abraham). And Abraham's claim is a lesser one than that of Moses, who maintained that he was a messenger bringing God's law to the world. Even

...Key Religious Leaders

Divine Confirmation of Key Claims	Verification of Key Claims by Leader's Action and Fate	CONCLUSION Claims vs. Evidence
Evidence: Jewish writings. Miracles. Rating: ●●●●	Evidence: He was faithful, but sinful. He died. Rating: ●●●●	Claim was important and is backed by some archaeology. Jesus supported it.
Evidence: Jewish writings. Miracles. Many prophecies, 100-percent accurate. Rating: ●●●●●●	Evidence: He was faithful, but sinful. He died. Rating: ●●●●	Claim was very important and is backed by archaeological evidence, prophecy, and Jesus' words.
Evidence: Prophecy, eyewitnesses, history, miracles, archaeology. Rating: ●●●●●●●	Evidence: He was sinless. He died, but rose again. Rating: ●●●●●●●	Most important claim of all— to be God incarnate. Backed by substantial evidence of all kinds.
Evidence: The "beautiful language" of the Qur'an. Rating: ●	Evidence: Performed good actions but incited rebellion. He died. Rating: ●●●	Very important claim backed by archaeology, but not by clear divine evidence.
Evidence: None. Rating: -	Evidence: A politician that united his country on ethical values. He died. Rating: ●●	Claim was of limited value— a philosophy of life. Political. Moral teaching.
Evidence: None. Rating: -	Evidence: We don't know the history of the Hindu leaders. Rating: ●	Claims affect many people with teaching about the afterlife. No evidence supporting inspiration.
Evidence: None Rating: -	Evidence: He was apparently genuinely concerned for his people's welfare. He died. Rating: ●●	Claims affect many people with teaching about the afterlife. No evidence supporting inspiration.
Evidence: None. Rating: -	Evidence: A deceiver who abused the trust of his followers. He died. Rating: -	Highly significant claim of godhood. Absolutely no evidence.
Evidence: None. Rating: -	Evidence: A recluse with harmful ideas who took advantage of others. He died. Rating: -	Claim of divine insight into Bible with no evidence.
Evidence: None. Rating: -	Evidence: Turned occult ideas into a reinvented gnostic religion. She died. Rating: -	Claim of an unbiblical god and Jesus. Evidence strongly contradicts doctrine.
Evidence: None. Rating: -	Evidence: Apparently started his religion for personal financial gain. Deceptive. Rating: -	A "science-fiction" religion with no basis in factual evidence. Deceives people.

Value: Supremely significant: ●●●●●●●
Extremely significant: ●●●●●●
Very significant: ●●●●●
Somewhat significant: ●●●●
Significant: ●●●
Possibly significant: ●●
Significance low: ●
Zero or negative value: -

Moses' claim pales in comparison beside Jesus' claim to actually be God. Furthermore, claims are one thing, and evidence supporting them is another. Hopefully this basic guide will encourage everyone to make his or her own "ratings" and judgments about leaders of religions.

Hindu Leaders

Hinduism centers in India, the world's second most populous nation, whose population is about 82 percent Hindu. Strictly defined, the followers of Hinduism make up about 13 percent of the world's population. However, it has a much more far-reaching impact because it forms the basis for the "Christian" mind-science cults (for example, Christian Science); New Age religions and practices (transcendental meditation, for instance); and other philosophies and religions as well. Furthermore, Buddhism resulted from Gautama Buddha's reforms of Hinduism.

History [3,4,5]

There is no single leader who has been identified as the founder of Hinduism. In fact, the religion has many variants, any of which may have had its own founder. Hinduism is one of the world's oldest religions, dating back to about 1500 B.C. Its doctrines and variations developed over a period of centuries, as did its holy books and writings.

Beliefs and Doctrines [3,4,5]

Major Beliefs: Several doctrines are consistent through all Hindu sects.

Brahma—The impersonal life-force within all things; "god."

Karma—The concept of moral cause and effect, or "you reap what you sow." Considered to be an actual "force."

Caste system—People are born to different statuses in life, depending upon their karma from past lives.

Reincarnation—A cycle of successive rebirths enabling people to work off their karma and eventually to reach the ultimate dissolution that brings them freedom from the cycle.

Dharma—The moral order that people must follow to eliminate karma.

God: "God" is an impersonal force; an undefinable, all-pervading deity. Hinduism recognizes hundreds, even thousands, of lesser gods.

Mankind: People are morally neutral, but their status reflects their karma from past lives, which they must work off in order to reach nirvana.

Sin: Actions and thoughts inconsistent with dharma, the moral order. "Sin" does not affect a person's relationship to Brahman.

Jesus: He is not an issue.

Salvation: Nirvana can be achieved by working off karma through actions, knowledge, or devotion on the part of an individual. Working off karma to achieve nirvana—the state of dissolution—may require millions of reincarnations.

Leadership Issues

Since we do not know who the founders of Hinduism are, we cannot examine their lives and actions. However, many modern leaders of variants of Hinduism, New Age religions, and mind-science cults have had enormous problems with personal credibility and honesty.

Fate of Hindu leaders: All known leaders in Hinduism and of Hinduism-based religions who have died have remained dead.

Leader:	No identified founder
Dates:	Founded about 1500 B.C.
Holy Writings:	The Vedas
	The Mahabharata
	The Ramayana
	The Bhagavad-Gita
Key Claims:	Great variation:
	Work your way to nirvana through successive reincarnations
	Religions are all related
	There are many paths to god
Key Evidence:	Philosophy
Divine Evidence:	None

Buddha (Buddhism)

Buddhism currently claims about six percent of the world's population,[5] and is sometimes combined with other major religions (mainly Confucianism or Shintoism). Two of the major sects of Buddhism are *Theravada,* which is based on the original form of Buddha's teachings and is prevalent in southern Asia; and *Mahayana,* which centers in China and Japan. Theravada Buddhism emphasizes the individuality of humans and the necessity of self-effort to achieve salvation, which is limited to the worthy; Mahayana stresses social concern and people's interdependence, accepts many writings as scripture, and teaches that everyone will receive the "grace" necessary for salvation.[3,4,5]

History[3,4,5]

Buddha, originally named Siddhartha Gautama, was born in 563 B.C. in a part of northern India that is now part of Nepal. Tradition says that Buddha was sheltered by his family in a palace so that he would never see the enormous suffering in the world from old age, sickness, poverty, and death. One day, Buddha ventured out and encountered all these forms of suffering, which inspired him to devote his life to discovering the source of suffering and finding a way to eliminate it. After six years of extreme self-denial, he realized that self-induced suffering would not bring him enlightenment. He then ate some food and sat under a fig tree to meditate, vowing not to rise until he was enlightened. After a time, he asserted that he had received the enlightenment he was seeking, and he became the "Buddha," which means "the enlightened one."

The Teachings of Buddhism[3,4,5]

Main Groups: *Theravada* puts emphasis on the necessity of the individual to achieve enlightenment through worthy acts. Enlightenment is not granted to all. *Mahayana* teaches universal salvation and the mutual interdependence of people. *Vajrayana* (a third Buddhist sect) is closest to Hinduism and centers on occult practices.

God: God is an abstract. In essence, Buddhism is an atheistic philosophy.

Man: We suffer because of our desires for temporary things.

Sin: Suffering is the focus, not sin as such.

Jesus: He is not a factor.

Salvation: Total enlightenment brings us to nirvana, a state of blessedness in which all desire and individual consciousness is extinguished.

Leadership Issues

Though Buddha was later deified by some of his followers, he never professed to be a god. He didn't pretend to be something he was not, but attempted to improve upon Hindu philosophy, based upon his discoveries from his personal "enlightenment."

The Fate of Buddha:
He died about the year 483 B.C. and remained dead.

Key Leader:	Buddha
Dates:	563 to 483 B.C.
Holy Writings:	The "Three Baskets" (The Pali Scriptures) (The Mahayana canon is open and contains many holy writings)
Key Claims:	Moral conduct for enlightenment: Take no life Do not steal Remain sexually moral Do not tell falsehoods Do not take intoxicants
Key Evidence:	Philosophy
Divine Evidence:	None

Joseph Smith (Mormonism)

Joseph Smith was the founder of the "Church of Jesus Christ of Latter-Day Saints," the largest branch of which is known as Mormons. With a membership of several million, the Mormons are one of the largest "Christian" cults. However, this membership is far less than one percent of the world's population and does not begin to compare in size to biblical Christianity.

History[4,5,6,7,8,9]

Joseph Smith was a mystic and a treasure-seeker (he apparently spent years looking for the buried treasure of Captain Kidd). He became known as a practicer of occult-type rituals, which eventually resulted in his imprisonment in 1826. Smith denounced all religions and claimed he had received visions from the angel "Moroni" in 1820 and 1823 that directed him to buried "golden plates." From the writing on these plates he claimed to have translated the *Book of Mormon*. These plates have never been seen by anyone else.

The *Book of Mormon* and other Mormon writings have been extensively studied by experts. Among other findings, the historicity of the *Book of Mormon* has been flatly denied by representatives of the Smithsonian Institution; and the "Book of Abraham" in *Pearl of Great Price* was proven fraudulent by a Mormon expert in Egyptology. The failed prophecies of the Mormon writings have also caused problems for the church.*

In 1844, Joseph Smith was jailed for trying to stop press exposure of questionable Mormon activities. While he was awaiting trial, a mob broke into the prison and killed him. Mormon doctrine now teaches that Smith is a god who sits on the throne with Jesus and "Elohim" (another god, who was formerly a human); Smith will judge human beings along with these other gods.

---

* For instance, the *Book of Mormon* declares that Jesus' birth was to take place in Jerusalem (Alma 7:9,10), whereas it actually took place in Bethlehem. In several places, the *Doctrine and Covenants* asserts that western Missouri would be the site of "Zion" within one generation of 1832 and that "Zion" would never be moved from that place (D&C 84:1-5,31; 97:19; 101:17-21). This has never happened.

The Teaching of Mormonism[4,5,6,7,8,9]

God: God was once a man; any male can become a god. (Note: This doctrine is nowhere contained in *The Book of Mormon.*)

Mankind: People exist as spirits before birth and can become gods by adherence to church doctrines and rules in this life.

Sin: Doing approved works overcomes sin.

Jesus: A brother of Satan, created by "Elohim" through sexual union with Mary, who is one of Elohim's wives.

Salvation: Nearly everyone goes to some type of paradise. Those who strictly adhere to church rules achieve higher levels; males can even become gods.

Leadership Issues

Smith was dogged by controversy and questions about his personal integrity throughout his adult life. From all evidence, Smith deceived many people, though the Mormon church defends some of this as necessary for the founding and continuance of the "one true religion."

Leader: Joseph Smith

Dates: 1805 to 1844

Holy Writings: *The Book of Mormon*
Pearl of Great Price
Doctrine and Covenants
The Bible—the King James Version

Key Claims: God is simply an exalted man
Joseph Smith is a god
Smith, Jesus, and Elohim decide the fate of human beings

Key Evidence: None

Divine Evidence: None

The Fate of Joseph Smith: He died in 1844 and remained dead.

Charles Russell (Jehovah's Witnesses)

The Jehovah's Witnesses organization (the Watchtower Bible and Tract Society) was founded in the late 1800s by Charles Russell. This organization's teachings differ from biblical Christianity in many ways, most fundamentally in that the deity of Jesus is denied and His role is diminished. The Watchtower Society created a new "biblical" theology emphasizing that salvation is dependent upon our actions, and it places a high emphasis on prophecy about the end times.

History[4,5,6,7]

Charles Russell began his work in 1870 with a small group of Bible students, who in 1876 elected him "pastor." Russell later admitted in court that he had lied under oath regarding his knowledge of Greek, his ordination, and various other matters. It was on this foundation that the powerful Watchtower Society was founded in 1896. Russell centered his theological empire in Brooklyn, New York, where printing and publishing activities were carried on, housing was built, and stores of food were kept—much of the work done through volunteer labor.

After Russell's death in October, 1916, more was revealed about his character by a local newspaper which reported upon his litigation problems, the rocky course and breakup of his marriage, and his misappropriation of church funds to his own use—which implied that the Watchtower Society was actually a money-making venture for Russell.

Leader:	Charles Russell
Dates:	1852 to 1916
Holy Writings:	The "New World" Version of the Bible (a reworking of the King James Version) Watchtower writings
Key Claims:	Jesus was just a man
	Jesus did not physically rise from the dead
	Only 144,000 people have been saved; others must earn salvation by their deeds
Key Evidence:	None

The Society has now grown to the point where it has published *billions* of pieces of literature and sends millions of people out to convert others to Russell's teaching. Conversion is an activity that is pursued with particular zeal by Jehovah's Witnesses. However, the Society's membership has fluctuated greatly over the years because of disillusionment over its failed prophecies—in particular, its predictions about the end of the world.

The failure of prophecies is a problematic legacy for the Jehovah's Witnesses. The string of false predictions began with Russell's prediction of Jesus' "invisible" second coming in 1874, coupled with the end of the world in 1914. After this did not come about, the date of the end of the world was changed to 1918, then 1925, as were the dates for other future events. Finally, after many failures, the Watchtower Society seems to have given up on setting dates.

The Teaching of Charles Russell and the Jehovah's Witnesses[4,5,6,7]

God: He is called "Jehovah" and exists in a single person, unlike Christianity's one God in three persons. He never came to earth in the human form of Jesus.

Mankind: People are a material creation of Jehovah.

Sin: Sin can be overcome by one's good actions as defined by the Society.

Jesus: He is not divine, but rather is a creation of Jehovah—an angel who existed first as Michael, then as the man Jesus, and now exists again as Michael, the exalted angel.

Salvation: "The 144,000" have already been "saved." Everyone else must earn his or her way to good works, such as door-to-door proselytizing.

Leadership Issues

Charles Russell was not able to establish a credible reputation with people outside the Watchtower Society. The record shows that he deceived people and misused their good will for his own benefit.

The Fate of Charles Russell:
He died in 1916 and remained dead.

Mary Baker Eddy (Christian Science)

Christian Science is one of the leading "mind science" religions, all of which have a close relationship to the gnostic mystery religions of the first few centuries after Christ. Mary Baker Eddy based her doctrines on Phineas Parker Quimby's teachings about mental-psychic healing (Quimby was a New England psychic and spiritualist of the mid 1800s whom Eddy followed).

Christian Science and all gnostic beliefs are fundamentally opposed to biblical Christianity. They teach that only "mind" or "spirit" is real; "matter" is evil, being actually an illusion from which people must gain freedom—which they do by learning and studying special secrets, procedures, or "mysteries" (hence the term "mystery religions"). In accordance with this doctrinal system, Christian Science views sin, hell, and the biblical heaven as illusions. Everything ultimately depends on a person's "state of mind," which in turn is governed by a person's coming to understand that "god" is in everyone and part of everything.

History[4,5,6,7,10,11]

The gnostic heresies (which were condemned by the apostles Paul and John in the first century) were reintroduced in modern form by Phineas Parker Quimby. Mary Baker Eddy made free use of Quimby's ideas in her own writings about the "God is mind" philosophy in 1866. Eddy had been a spiritist medium for about 25 years when she claimed to have discovered Christian Science principles after a near brush with death (her report of her medical condition was, however,

Leader:	Mary Baker Eddy
Dates:	1821 to 1910
Holy Writings:	The Bible
	Science and Health
Key Claims:	Jesus was just a man
	His crucifixion was meaningless
	Jesus did not physically rise from the dead
	Everyone has god in him ("Christ consciousness")
	Real sin and hell don't exist
	Matter is an illusion
Key Evidence:	None
Divine Evidence:	None

disputed by the attending physician). Eddy's doctrines focus on the "science of mind" and claim to "go beyond the Bible" in the book *Science and Health with Key to the Scriptures*. This book is used by Christian Scientists as a guide to interpreting the Bible.

The first tenet of Christian Science is: "...We take the inspired Word of the Bible as our sufficient guide to eternal life." However, Christian Science rejects the role of Jesus and existence of sin and hell, all of which are clearly proclaimed in the Bible. How do its followers reconcile this conflict? They attempt to do so by their method of "Bible study." People are urged to first read a passage from the Bible, a practice that seems to lend the Bible's credibility to Christian Science; but then they are instructed to read the commentary on the scriptural passage from *Science and Heath*. Often there is little in common, but people begin to build their belief systems upon the teachings from *Science and Health*.

The Teaching of Mary Baker Eddy and Christian Science[4,5,6,7,10,11]

God: God is an impersonal, all-pervasive spirit that is in everyone. All people are part God.

Man: People are spirits, but are bound by the illusion that they are made up of matter.

Sin: Sin is merely blindness—ignorance of the fact that people are spirit, not matter.

Jesus: Jesus was simply a highly enlightened Christian Scientist. The "Christ" refers to an advanced state of consciousness that everyone has to some degree— "Jesus more than others."

Salvation: Salvation is a process of learning to slough off the illusion that we are material. Since there is no fall from grace, no hell, and no Satan as the Bible teaches, there is no need to be "redeemed" from anything.

Leadership Issues

Mary Baker Eddy actually rejected the teachings of the Bible although she stated that it was the "sufficient guide to eternal life." This is representative of the inconsistencies that her life and teaching exhibited.

The Fate of Mary Baker Eddy:
She died in December, 1910 and remained dead.

L. Ron Hubbard (Scientology)

Among the most unusual doctrinal systems is the religion of Scientology. Born from the mind of science fiction writer L. Ron Hubbard, Scientology promotes belief in an extraterrestrial race called "Thetans" and offers special supernatural treatments that can provide salvation—at substantial expense. Among those people who have been attracted to this religion are the confused, the emotionally and mentally ill, and several prominent Hollywood actors (including Karen Black, John Travolta, and Lou Rawls). Governments of several countries have investigated Scientology and have warned their citizens about the truthfulness of its claims. In the United States, church offices have been raided by the FBI; the organization has been investigated by the FDA and the IRS; and it continues to be embroiled in many lawsuits over its activities.[4,5,6,7]

History[4,5,6,7]

L. Ron Hubbard was born in 1911. He graduated from George Washington University with a degree in nuclear physics (though transcripts show he was on academic probation and had failed the subject of physics). He maintained that he had a Ph.D. from Sequoia University in California, though no such accredited institution could be found. Before becoming a religious leader, Hubbard was a successful science fiction writer; his ideas led eventually to the writing of the bestselling book *Dianetics: The Modern Science of Mental Health,* which launched the "religion" of Scientology.

Leader:	L. Ron Hubbard
Period:	1911 to 1986
Holy Writings:	*Dianetics*
	Various other publications
Key Claims:	L. Ron Hubbard had "special enlightenment"
	All people's souls are god
	Reincarnation helps people become "Thetan"
	Treatments help people to a higher status
	The Bible is useless
Key Evidence:	None
Divine Evidence:	None

An entire program was developed around the existence of trillion-year-old aliens called Thetans. Treatments were developed to remove "engrams" (scars from psychic-spiritual traumas) from patients' minds so that the Thetans could have free rein within the people's spirits. Scientology claims to have a floating "hospital ship" that can be concealed from public and governmental knowledge; it is supposedly in this ship that the treatments are carried out. Some deaths have been documented as a result of treatment for the removal of "engrams." During the rise of Scientology, Hubbard became a millionaire and a recluse; he died in 1986.

The Teachings of Scientology[4,5,6,7]

God: "God" as such is irrelevant. All people's souls are gods.

Man: People are essentially good, but must be reincarnated until the godlike "Thetan" status is realized.

Sin: Human reason will produce perfect behavior. The Bible is useless. It is "beneath contempt to tell a man he must repent, that he is evil."

Jesus: An advanced human who had a "strong energy glow" but was not at the "highest operating Thetan" level.

Salvation: There is no hell to be saved from, but freedom from the cycle of reincarnation can be achieved, especially if proper treatments—at a considerable cost—are undertaken.

Leadership Issues

Hubbard profited immensely from the religion he created. Many mentally and emotionally impaired people have been further injured by their participation in Scientology.

The fate of L. Ron Hubbard:
He died in 1986 and has remained dead.

Jesus Fulfilled Prophecy from God

Not one of the previously discussed religious leaders was mentioned beforehand in prophecy—except Jesus. Not one detail of any of their lives was predicted by divinely inspired prophecy—except for the details of Jesus' life. In fact, study of the life of *any* religious leader—from any period in history—will reveal that *only Jesus' life was precisely foretold by divine prophecy.*

A Vast Number of Prophecies Were Made About Jesus

If we were to select just 48 of the prophecies about Jesus and calculate the odds of their being fulfilled in one single man, we would find that those odds would be *much more remote* than the odds of picking a single designated electron out of the entire contents of the universe![12]

All of the following prophecies were made at least 400 years before Jesus' birth and were fulfilled by Him:

Prophecy	Fulfillment
• The Redeemer lives, would be victorious in the end (Job 19:25-27)	Jesus in history
• The Messiah* would descend from Abraham (Genesis 12:3)	Matthew 1, Luke 3
• The Messiah would descend from Isaac (Genesis 22:18; 26:4)	Matthew 1, Luke 3
• The Messiah would descend from Jacob (Genesis 28:14)	Matthew 1, Luke 3
• The Messiah would descend from Judah (Genesis 49:10-12)	Matthew 1, Luke 3
• No bones of Messiah would be broken (Exodus 12:46)	John 19:31-36
• The Messiah would be raised up as a great prophet like Moses (Deuteronomy 18:15-19)	John 6:14
• The Messiah would be hung on a tree and become a curse on behalf of His people (Deuteronomy 21:23)	Galatians 3:13
• The Holy One would not see decay (Psalm 16:1-10)	Matthew 28
• Crucifixion: many details given (Psalm 22)	Matthew 27, Mark 15
• False witnesses would accuse God's Anointed One (Psalm 27:12)	Matthew 26:59-61
• The Anointed One would say, "into your hands I commit my spirit" (Psalm 31:3-5)	Luke 23:46
• No bones of "the righteous man" would be broken (Psalm 34:20)	John 19:36

* Note: The Hebrew word *Messiah* means "anointed one."

- The Messiah would be hated without cause (Psalm 35:19) .... John 15:24,25
- His friends would stay far away (Psalm 38:11) .... Matthew 27:55
- The Anointed One would be betrayed by a friend
  (Psalm 41:9) .... Matthew 26:14-16
- The Anointed One would be scorned by his enemies
  (Psalm 69:9, 19) .... Romans 15:3
- The Anointed One would be given gall and vinegar
  (Psalm 69:21) .... Matthew 27:34,48
- The Lord's "son" would be a descendant of Solomon
  and rule forever (2 Samuel 7:12-14) .... Matthew 1
- The teacher would speak in parables (Psalm 78:2) .... Matthew 13:34,35
- Some Jews (the "builders") would reject the Anointed One
  (Psalm 118:22) .... Matthew 21:42
- The Anointed One would be a descendant of David
  and rule forever (Psalm 132:11,12) .... Matthew 1, Luke 3
- "The boy" would be born of a virgin (Isaiah 7:14-16) .... Matthew 1:18-23
- "Special" miracles would accompany the coming of the
  Anointed One (Isaiah 35:4-6) .... Matthew 15:30,31
- There would be a forerunner to the Anointed One
  (Isaiah 40:1-5) .... Matthew 3:1-3
- Description of the actions of the "Lord" (Isaiah 42:1-13) .... History
- The Lord's "Servant" to redeem Israel would also be a
  "light to the Gentiles" (Isaiah 49:6) .... Luke 2:28-33
- The Lord's "Servant" would be obedient in His time
  of humiliation (Isaiah 50) .... Matthew 26:59–27:35
- The Lord's "Righteous Servant" would be a suffering servant (Isaiah 53) . History
- The "Righteous Servant" would die along with evil men and be
  buried among the rich (Isaiah 53:9) .... Mark 15:27,43-46
- The Lord's "Son" would be called out of Egypt (Hosea 11:1) .. Matthew 2:14,15
- The "Ruler over Israel" who had existed "from ancient times"
  would come from Bethlehem (Micah 5:1-4) .... Matthew 2:1-6
- The "Anointed One, the Ruler" would come 173,880 days from the
  decree to rebuild the temple and Jerusalem (Daniel 9:25) .... Matthew 21:1-11
- Jerusalem would rejoice over the king who would come
  on a donkey (Zechariah 9:9) .... Matthew 21:4,5
- The betrayer of the "flock" of Israel would be paid
  30 pieces of silver (Zechariah 11:12,13) .... Matthew 26:14,15
- The Lord would be "pierced" (said before crucifixion
  was invented) (Zechariah 12:10) .... John 19:34-37

Jesus Claimed to Be God

Many times Jesus either unequivocally asserted that He was God or made statements and performed actions that implied the same thing. His words and actions so infuriated the religious leaders of the day that they tried several times to kill him for "blasphemy" (claiming that He was God); eventually they succeeded in putting Him into the hands of the Roman government, which crucified Him.

If we look at Jesus' actions and words, we can see four specific ways in which He indicated that He was divine:

1. Jesus indicated that He could forgive sins.

The Jews believed that only the single God of the universe could forgive sins. When Jesus made this claim, the religious leaders said that he was blaspheming (Matthew 9:1-8—see below for more about this incident).

2. Jesus accepted worship.

In the law of Moses, God specifically commanded the Israelites to worship only Him. Jesus demonstrated that He was in fact God by accepting the worship of, among others, His disciples (Luke 5:8; John 20:28).

3. Jesus specifically said that He was God.

Besides the examples given on the next page, Jesus said "I and the Father are one" (John 10:30). He also told the religious leaders, "Before Abraham was born, I am!" (John 8:58—"I am" was one of the names that God used of Himself). The leaders clearly recognized what Jesus was saying and started to pick up stones to stone Him for blasphemy.

4. Jesus performed miracles that only God could do.

Jesus did the same miracles that Isaiah had prophesied would be signs of God's presence (Isaiah 35:4-6).

Here are some fuller examples of Jesus' actions and claims:

- He forgave the sins of a man who had been paralyzed since birth. The religious leaders recognized His action as either evidence that He was God ("only God can forgive sins")—or blasphemy. Jesus silenced them by healing the paralyzed man in front of them and other witnesses—a miracle that only God could perform (Matthew 9:1-8).

- The Jewish religious laws forbade the gathering of food or the performing of any work at all on the Sabbath (Saturday), which was a ceremonial day of rest that God had commanded. On one Sabbath, Jesus allowed His disciples to pick some wheat to satisfy their hunger; He also healed a man with a deformed hand. When the religious leaders tried to condemn Him, He proclaimed that He was "Lord of the Sabbath"—indicating that He was equal to the One who had created the Sabbath. The religious leaders began plotting to kill Him after this (Matthew 12:1-14).

- Jesus called Himself the "capstone" (the highest and most critical part of a building) that was rejected by the "builders"—in this case the religious leaders. Again they tried to find a way to arrest Him (Matthew 21:42-46).

- At His final trial, when Jesus was asked whether He was the "Christ, the Son of God," He replied that He was. At this point the high priest tore his own clothes—a sign of great distress over, among other things, blasphemy—and the religious leaders emphatically demanded that Jesus die for His "blasphemy" (Matthew 26:63-66).

Jesus' Miracles Were a Sign

The Jewish religious tradition regarded certain miracles as indication of God's presence. They included making the blind see, the lame walk, the deaf hear; the curing of leprosy; and the raising of the dead. Isaiah listed several of these miracles as those that would occur when "your God will come" (Isaiah 35:4-6). Jesus did all these things, many times in the presence of numerous witnesses, and later spoke of these same miracles when confirming His deity to John the Baptist (Matthew 11:2-5).

Jesus Proved He Was God

How can anyone prove he is God? According to God's words in the Bible, there is literally only one way that Jesus or anyone else can prove He is God:

1. **Demonstrate first that he is a prophet of God by proclaiming perfect fulfilled prophecy.**

   Only God can predict the future (Isaiah 46:10). The Bible tell us to "test everything" (1 Thessalonians 5:21) and specifically tells us to use prophecy as the test of something that is alleged to come from God (Deuteronomy 18:14-22).

2. **Then prophesy that he is God—and that he will prove it by performing a miracle that only God can perform.**

   In addition to maintaining that He was God (see pages 38, 39), Jesus told both His disciples and the Jewish religious leaders that He would be *resurrected from the dead*, which would be a confirmation of all His words and prophecies.

3. **Finally, fulfill the prophecy and perform the miracle that he predicted.**

   Jesus fulfilled His prophecy of the miracle of the resurrection. *The resurrection verified His claim to be God* and confirmed His triumph over death.

Prophecies About Jesus

Jesus specifically fulfilled more than 100 prophecies (some of these are listed on pages 36, 37). This is in itself amazing and indicates God's involvement. Statistically speaking, it would be impossible for one individual to fulfill all these prophecies by chance—it indicates that God must have planned the fulfillment. People recognized God's hand in Jesus' life even before His death; for instance, at the beginning of Jesus' public work, John the Baptist hailed Jesus as "the Lamb of God, who takes away the sin of the world" and as the "Son of God" (John 1:29,34).

But for Jesus to clearly demonstrate His deity, He needed to make a specific prophecy regarding His claim to deity. The fulfillment of the prophecy would have to be irrefutable and would have to require a miracle that only God could perform, thus demonstrating that Jesus was God's "anointed one" (Messiah). This ultimate prophecy, a prediction that only God could make, was Jesus' prophecy of His death and resurrection (resurrection being something that only God could do).

Jesus *accurately prophesied the miracle of His resurrection* several times, in several different ways. At least three times He told His disciples that He would be executed but would rise again in three days (Matthew 16:21; 17:22,23; 20:17-19). He also made this prediction to the religious leaders, referring to Jonah's three-day captivity inside the great fish as a model of His own three-day captivity within the grave (Matthew 16:4).

There was absolutely no doubt that Jesus' prophecy about His resurrection after three days was widely known and regarded as important. For instance, the religious leaders approached Pilate (the Roman governor) after Jesus' death, asking that Pilate take extra precautions to make the tomb secure so that the disciples couldn't contrive a false resurrection (Matthew 27:62-66).

We should also note that Jesus prophesied several more things during His last days:

- He would be betrayed by a friend—He also indicated which friend would betray Him (Matthew 26:21-25)
- Peter would disown Him (John 13:37,38)
- Jerusalem would be besieged and torn down (Luke 19:41-44—fulfilled in A.D. 69 and 70)
- He would return to Galilee (Mark 14:28)

The Miracle of the Resurrection

Jesus precisely prophesied His own miraculous resurrection from the dead. He made no errors in any other predictions that He made. Furthermore, He professed to be God. And God tells us to use prophecy as a test to know whether something is from Him. Therefore, *the prophecies Jesus made, along with their fulfillment by the events of His death and resurrection, verify His claim to be God.*

History Confirms Jesus' Deity

Religious leaders other than Jesus have made major doctrinal claims about issues such as life after death—but have given *no* evidence that the information was from God.

Jesus was unique, in that He claimed to be God and proved He was God.

Therefore, if Jesus is God, He clearly is able to speak for God on matters concerning both this life and the hereafter. This issue demands that we look at the evidence for the events that support Jesus' credibility. If those events—His prophecy, His death, His resurrection—actually occurred, then all of Jesus' statements can be trusted. And it happens that we do have much evidence for the historicity of these events, from both Christian and non-Christian sources.

Eyewitness Accounts[4,13,14,15,16]

There were many eyewitnesses to the events of Jesus' life—His birth, His ministry, His death, and His resurrection. The Bible tells us that on one occasion after His resurrection, Jesus appeared to more than 500 people (1 Corinthians 15:6). Moreover, many of those people were still alive when the manuscripts containing such claims were circulating. If those letters and manuscripts had been false, the eyewitnesses would have denounced them as frauds.

We have a huge number—unequalled anywhere else—of ancient manuscripts that report the history of Jesus, including His remarkable predictions and His death and resurrection (some of these documents are from non-Christian sources). Many of these manuscripts are early copies of the letters and the Gospels. Amazingly, there still exist more than 24,000 of these ancient manuscript copies, in spite of centuries of efforts to eradicate the Christian Scriptures. Compare this to the number of surviving manuscripts of some of the great works of secular history, such as *The Gallic Wars* of Julius Caesar. Only ten copies remain of this work, yet its historicity is never questioned.

This type of hard, factual manuscript evidence doesn't even apply in the case of other religious leaders. Why? Because—

Other religious leaders were *alone* at the time they
alleged they were "inspired."

Consider Buddha, under the fig tree—alone. Or Muhammad, in
his "place of solitude." Or Confucius. Or Joseph Smith during his
purported encounter with Moroni. Any of these leaders could
write anything they wanted and claim they were given divine revelation—and no one could contradict them. On the other hand,
there were many witnesses to the events of Jesus' life, which
fulfilled both ancient prophecies and Jesus' own predictions.

The History of the Early Church Confirms the Events of Jesus' Life[4,13,14,15,16]

There is an enormous body of historical documents that supports
the fact that thousands of early Christians willingly suffered ex-
ecution—often of the most horrible kind—because they *refused to
deny the historical fact of Jesus' death and resurrection.* This is most
significant because Jesus' claim to be God was based on *prior
prophecy* that was fulfilled by *historical events.* Other martyrs sometimes die for unprovable philosophies or for lesser causes. But
among the first martyrs of the Christian church were Jesus' own
disciples, who would certainly have known the truth and would
not have died for a "resurrection lie." All of the original apostles,
according to historical tradition, were executed in horrible ways
(except John). They were not willing to back away from the historical facts of Jesus' miraculous prophecy, His death, and His
resurrection.

Jesus confirmed that He was God in human flesh.

Confirmation from Archaeology

Ossuaries (tombs for bones) dated to a few years after Jesus' death
have been found just outside the city of Jerusalem. Inscriptions on
some of these ossuaries contain the phrases "Jesus, help" and "Jesus,
let him arise." Some of the people who buried their dead in these
tombs would have been alive during Jesus' lifetime—and they, likely
eyewitnesses to the events, considered Jesus to be God.

Conclusions and Questions

Jesus Is Vastly Different from Other Religious Leaders (see pages 6–9)

1. Jesus' claim was very special. He maintained that He was God in human flesh.

2. Jesus' claim was verified by prophecy and by the historical events of His death and resurrection.

3. Jesus' own prophecy, along with the divine miracle of the resurrection, provided evidence of God's involvement.

4. Jesus' pure, sinless life—in perfect accord with His teaching and His claims—supports His claim to be God.

How Can We Know Whether a Leader Is Really Leading Us Toward Jesus?

Many religious leaders profess to teach the truth about Jesus, or even to be "extensions" of Him, yet in reality they are far from Him. And some religious groups that call themselves "Christian" are not. It's important to be wise and careful in choosing whom you will meet with.* Here are a few guidelines:

1. Observe how often, and how clearly and accurately, the Bible is used in teaching.

2. Is Jesus referred to as God and as part of the Trinity (Father, Son, and Holy Spirit)?

3. Who is being glorified—Jesus? Or some other individual or thing?

4. Does the group believe that Jesus was crucified to provide forgiveness and redemption from sin?

5. Does the group believe that Jesus was physically raised from the dead, and that He was miraculously born from a virgin?

---

* Some of the references listed in the Notes and Bibliography can help guide you in your choice. You may also contact the Christian Research Institute at 949-858-6100, ext. 301 or at www.equip.org for information about a specific religious group or leader.

How Can We Ensure the Right Relationship So We Can Go to Heaven?

When Jesus said that not all people who use His name will enter heaven (Matthew 7:21-23), He was referring to people who think that using Christ's name along with rules and rituals is the key to heaven. A *relationship* with God is not based on rituals and rules. It's based on grace, forgiveness, and the right standing with Him through Jesus Christ.

How to Have a Personal Relationship with God

1. *Believe that God exists* and that He came to earth in the human form of Jesus Christ (John 3:16; Romans 10:9).

2. *Accept God's free forgiveness* of sins and gift of new life through the death and resurrection of Jesus Christ (Ephesians 2:8-10; 1:7,8).

3. *Switch to God's plan for your life* (1 Peter 1:21-23; Ephesians 2:1-7).

4. *Expressly make Jesus Christ the director* of your life (Matthew 7:21-27; 1 John 4:15).

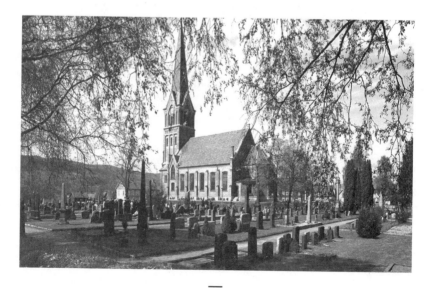

Prayer for Eternal Life with God

"Dear God, I believe You sent Your Son, Jesus, to die for my sins so I can be forgiven. I'm sorry for my sins, and I want to live the rest of my life the way You want me to. Please put Your Spirit in my life to direct me. Amen."

Then What?

People who sincerely take these steps become members of God's family of believers. A new world of freedom and strength is available through Jesus' life within you, expressing itself through prayer and obedience to God's will. The new relationship can be strengthened by taking the following steps:

- Find a Bible-based church that you like and attend regularly.
- Set aside some time each day to pray and read the Bible.
- Locate other Christians to spend time with on a regular basis.

God's Promises to Believers

For Today

But seek first his kingdom and his righteousness,
and all these things [things to satisfy all your needs]
will be given to you as well.
—*Matthew 6:33*

For Eternity

Whoever believes in the Son has eternal life,
but whoever rejects the Son will not see life,
for God's wrath remains on him.
—*John 3:36*

Once we develop an eternal perspective, even the greatest problems on earth fade in significance.

Notes

Note: The author does not recommend several references below that were necessary in order to test all viewpoints. (*"Test everything"* —1 Thessalonians 5:21).

1. *Webster's II New Riverside University Dictionary*, Riverside, CA: The Riverside Publishing Company, 1976.

2. Draper, Edythe (Editor), *Almanac of the Christian World*, Wheaton, IL: Tyndale House Publishers, Inc., 1992.

3. Halverson, Dean, *The Compact Guide to World Religions*, Minneapolis, MN: Bethany House, 1996.

4. Geisler, Norman, Ph.D, *Baker Encyclopedia of Christian Apologetics*, Grand Rapids, MI: Baker Books, 1999. [highly recommended]

5. McDowell, Josh, *Handbook of Today's Religions*, San Bernardino, CA: Campus Crusade for Christ, 1983. [highly recommended]

6. Martin, Walter, *The Kingdom of the Cults*, Minneapolis, MN: Bethany House, 1996. [highly recommended]

7. Ankerberg, John, and Weldon, John, *Encyclopedia of Cults and New Religions*, Eugene, OR: Harvest House, 1999. [highly recommended]

8. Bodine, Jerry and Marian, *Witnessing to Mormons*, Rancho Santa Margarita, CA: Christian Research Institute, 1978. [highly recommended]

9. *Book of Mormon, Doctrine and Covenants, Pearl of Great Price*, Salt Lake City, UT: Church of Jesus Christ of Latter Day Saints, 1981. [not recommended]

10. *Christian Science Quarterly—Weekly Bible Lessons*, Boston, MA: Christian Science Publishing Company, January–March, 2000. [not recommended]

11. Eddy, Mary Baker, *Science and Health*, Boston, MA: Published by the Trustees Under the Will of Mary Baker Eddy, 1906. [not recommended]

12. Stoner, Peter, *Science Speaks*, Chicago, IL: Moody Press, 1963.

13. McDowell, Josh, and Wilson, Bill, *A Ready Defense*, San Bernardino, CA: Here's Life Publishers, Inc., 1990.

14. Muncaster, Ralph O., *How Do We Know Jesus Is God?*, Eugene, OR: Harvest House, 2000.

15. Muncaster, Ralph O., *What Really Happened Christmas Morning?*, Eugene, OR: Harvest House, 2000.

16. Geisler, Norman, Ph.D, and Brooks, Ron, *When Skeptics Ask*, Grand Rapids, MI: Baker Books, 1990.

17. Smith, Jay (from the debate "Who Is the True Jesus?" presented by the Master of Arts Program in Christian Apologetics at Biola University in La Mirada, CA, on October 23, 2000).

Bibliography

Dawood, NJ., (Translator), *The Koran*, New York, NY: Penguin Books, 1993. [not recommended]

Elwell, Walter A. (Editor), *Evangelical Dictionary of Theology*, Grand Rapids, MI: Baker Book House Co., 1984. [highly recommended]

Life Application Bible, Wheaton, IL: Tyndale House Publishers, and Grand Rapids, MI: Zondervan Publishing House, 1991.

Muncaster, Ralph O., *Does the Bible Predict the Future?*, Eugene, OR: Harvest House, 2000.

Walvoord, John F., *The Prophecy Knowledge Handbook*, Wheaton, IL: Victor Books, 1990.

Watson, William, *A Concise Dictionary of Cults & Religions*, Chicago, IL: Moody, 1991.

Youngblood, Ronald F., *New Illustrated Bible Dictionary*, Nashville, TN: Nelson, 1995